EPSOM
TO HORSHAM

Vic Mitchell and Keith Smith

Cover design – Deborah Goodridge
ISBN 0 906520 30 4

First published April 1986

© *Middleton Press, 1986.*

Published by Middleton Press
         Easebourne Lane
         Midhurst, West Sussex.
         GU29 9AZ
         ☎ *073 081 3169*

Typeset by CitySet · Bosham 573270

Printed & bound by Biddles Ltd,
         Guildford and Kings Lynn.

CONTENTS

GEOGRAPHICAL SETTING

The route first crosses the light sandy soils of Epsom and Ashtead Commons before entering the Mole Gap in the North Downs. South of Dorking the line tunnels through the Hythe Beds of the Lower Greensand from where it climbs onto the Wealden Clay. Near Ockley the watershed between the tributaries of the north flowing Mole and south flowing Arun is reached. The descent ends a mile before Horsham, which stands on the slightly elevated western extremity of the Hastings Beds.

ACKNOWLEDGEMENTS

We would like to express our appreciation of the assistance received from the photographers mentioned in the captions and also help received from Mrs. E. Fisk, J. Harrod, N. Langridge, R.C. Riley, R. Randell, N. Stanyon, D. Wallis and our wives. Our thanks also go to Mrs. E.M. Wallis for permission to use photographs by the late E. Wallis and to members of the Brighton Circle for LBSCR information.

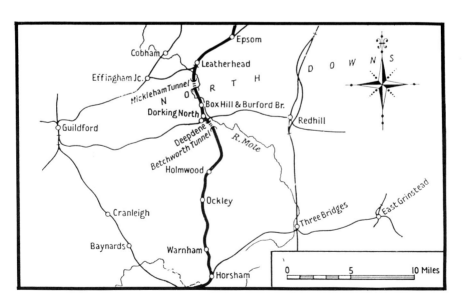

(Railway Magazine)

HISTORICAL BACKGROUND

Railway development in the area in the 1840s consisted of a London Brighton & South Coast Railway branch to Epsom (opened on 10th May 1847); the South Eastern Railway's east-west line through Dorking in 1849 and a LBSCR branch from Three Bridges to Horsham on 14th February 1848. The latter was extended to Petworth in 1859.

The London & South Western Railway reached Epsom from Wimbledon on 4th April 1859. It also acquired the line, then under construction, to Leatherhead, but arranged to work it jointly with the LBSCR, although they built separate stations at that town. LSWR services commenced on 1st February 1859, the LBSCR following on 8th August 1859.

The LBSCR started running trains to Dorking on 11th March 1867, extending services to Horsham on 1st May of that year.

The LSWR commenced operation between Leatherhead and Effingham Junction on 2nd February 1885, to link up with its new line to Guildford.

Electrification from Epsom to Leatherhead and on to Guildford took place on 12th July 1925. The third rail was extended to Horsham and the South Coast on 3rd July 1938.

During World War II, the Southern Railway moved its headquarters to Dorking, occupying the now-demolished Deepdene Hotel.

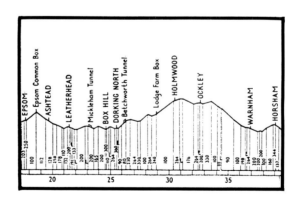

PASSENGER SERVICES

By 1869, the LBSCR was providing three trains on the full length of the route on weekdays, with an extra evening service from London to Ockley. Sundays brought only two trains each way. At that time, there were an additional nine weekday journeys as far south as Dorking with the LSWR providing 10 trains on weekdays between Leatherhead and "Waterloo Bridge" (four on Sundays).

In 1890, the LSWR were running 14 weekday and 4 Sunday trains, half of which ran to or from Guildford. The LBSCR were providing 10 trains stopping at most stations down to Horsham, with 3 on Sundays. By then there were also five Portsmouth expresses, mostly running non-stop on this section of the route. The local service between London and Dorking consisted of 7 weekday trips, with 6 on Sundays.

Twenty years later the LSWR service had increased to 18 weekday trains, 9 of which ran to Effingham Junction or beyond. The LBSCR local service had also increased, but the Portsmouth trains remained much the same.

In 1924, the Waterloo service was basically hourly, running as far as Horsley. The former LBSCR services were concentrated mainly on Victoria and comprised ten stopping trains to Dorking, ten to Horsham and seven expresses to the South Coast.

The introduction of electric traction brought regular interval services. For many years, the timetable to Effingham Junction showed a Waterloo and London Bridge service each hour, supplemented by an additional Waterloo train each hour after World War II. Reduction to two an hour took place about 1960 and since May 1971 there has been an hourly Waterloo service only, except in peak hours.

Electrified services in 1938 south of Leatherhead comprised of hourly trains between Victoria and Bognor Regis/Portsmouth; Victoria and Holmwood; Victoria and Dorking; and London Bridge and Dorking. During World War II services were often curtailed in off-peak times, but a special daily train of two 2NOLs ran to Dorking for railway staff transferred to work at the Deepdene Hotel.

The post war years saw a similar pattern of operation, but Holmwood termination was restricted to the rush hours only and was finally ended in 1976. Many of the fast trains to the South Coast ran via Three Bridges, but in 1965 these once again called hourly at Sutton, Dorking and Horsham. These were supplemented by an hourly Waterloo - Horsham service until 4th May 1969, after which date this stopping service terminated at Dorking. Holmwood, Ockley and Warnham have since only been served by trains in the business hours. In 1979 all coastal services were diverted to call at Gatwick Airport, except one or two, in the morning and evening, but even these ceased in 1984.

EPSOM

1. This is the exterior of the LBSCR station which was ⅜-mile east of the present one and became Epsom Town under Southern Railway ownership. It was closed to passengers on 3rd March 1929 and will be illustrated more fully in a future album. (Pamlin Prints)

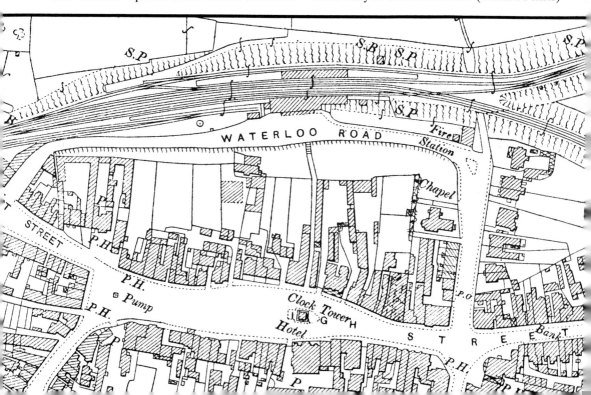

2. The LSWR arrived in the town 12 years after its competitor and whilst its station was built at the junction of their lines, the track layout was designed to prevent LBSCR trains calling at the platforms. In 1923, the SR inherited this unsatisfactory arrangement and this 1926 photograph, taken on 2nd October, shows a train from Epsom Town passing over the junction. The locomotive is class D1 no.B359. (H.C. Casserley)

1896 map. At this time there were undeveloped fields to the north of the railway. The layout of the lines prevented LBSCR trains from Sutton calling at this LSWR station.

3. Class R1 no.A706 runs south on the same day, as two pairs of Plus-fours amble north along the up platform. The platform roads have conductor rails, as the Waterloo services had been electrified in the previous year. (H.C. Casserley)

5. A view from the top of the up starting signal on 5th July 1928 shows that work had started on the reconstruction of the station. The up loop had been slewed away from the platform face on the right. (Late E. Wallis)

4. A third photograph taken that day shows a southbound express, hauled by ex-LBSCR class H1 4-4-0 no.41, running on the through line which avoided the LSWR platform. When scrapped in 1944, this 1906 locomotive had travelled 999,944 miles! (H.C. Casserley)

7. A view from the Sutton line Down Home signal four weeks later reveals the revised junction layout; the temporary footbridge; the new bridges over Waterloo Road; an electrical sub-station on the right; East Box in the centre and still peaceful fields in the background. A crop of semi-detached houses grew in them shortly afterwards.
(Late E. Wallis)

6. Looking south-west from the temporary footbridge on 10th February 1929, we see the new waiting room and offices on the left, the new overhead signal box in the centre, and the old vaulted canopy on the right.
(H.C. Casserley)

8. Looking in the opposite direction on the same day, one can see a carriage siding concrete walkway under construction on the right; a locomotive standing in the other carriage siding and West Box in the centre, behind which is the turntable siding.
(Late E. Wallis)

9. The new exterior presented a smart modern appearance in 1929. The Parcels Office is on the right. Two sidings and a dock were provided for parcel vans but all other goods traffic was retained at the former LBSCR station. (N. Langridge collection)

The 1932 map indicates the position of the locomotive turntable pit, the two dock sidings and the revised junction plan which gave convenient cross-platform interchange facilities for passengers.

The Folly

10. An unusual visitor on 4th October 1958 was ex-LSWR class T9 no.30120, hauling an RCTS railtour. It has subsequently become part of the National Railway Museum's collection and is currently in use on the Mid Hants Railway. Even earlier it had given your author (V.M.) much footplate pleasure when it was the regular shunting engine at Hampton, in the mid-1940s. (J. Scrace)

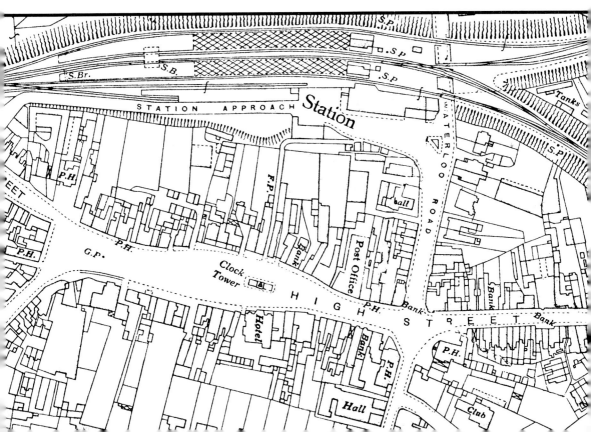

11. Epsom Common Box provided an intermediate block post until closed on 26th April 1964, most signals in the Epsom area being altered to colour lights by 1970. The locomotive is class C2X no.32544 and is seen in June 1961. (D. Clayton)

12. A well groomed class I3 gallops south with a Sunday excursion to Brighton in October 1932. The headcode indicates the London Bridge - Mitcham Junction route and not the destination. (Dr. I.C. Allen)

ASHTEAD

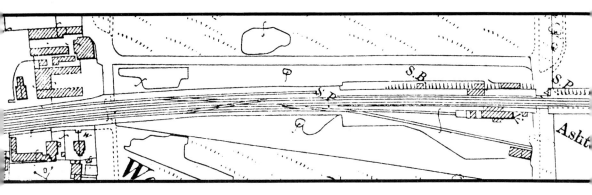

The 1895 map shows the arrangement before the sidings and platforms were lengthened and the two footbridges built.

13. Two features of interest in this view, from the footbridge towards Epsom, are the horse-drawn carriage in the station approach and the signal box on the platform. The latter was replaced by one at the end of the up platform which could control the gates at the road crossing, where traffic was increasing due to housing development north of the line. (J. Harrod collection)

14. An up express, probably from Portsmouth, runs through behind no.314 *Charles C. Macrae* on 19th August 1911. This 42-ton 4–4–0 had been rebuilt to class B2X four months earlier. The station master's house is on the right. (R.C. Riley collection)

1913

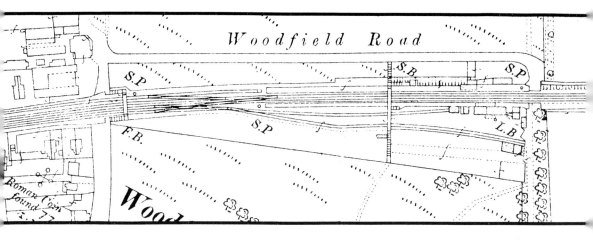

15. This 1959 photograph shows the final position of the signal box and also a dangerous staff crossing. Apart from the obvious danger of crossing running lines, this one is very narrow and there are no breaks in the conductor rail. (D. Cullum)

London & South Western Ry.
This Ticket is issued subject to the Regulations & Conditions stated in the Company's Time Tables & Bills

LEATHERHEAD to ASHTEAD

Leatherhead to Ashtead

3rd CLASS   (S.12)   3rd CLASS
Fare 2d   Fare 2d

674

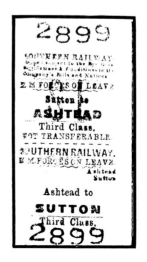

2899

SOUTHERN RAILWAY.
Issue subject to the Bye laws Regulations & Conditions in the Company's Bills and Notices

H. M. FORCES ON LEAVE

Sutton to
ASHTEAD
Third Class,
NOT TRANSFERABLE

SOUTHERN RAILWAY,
H.M.FORCES ON LEAVE
Ashtead
Sutton

Ashtead to
SUTTON
Third Class,
2899

16. A short goods train departs for Epsom in May 1961, hauled by class C2X no.32548. The parked cars subsequently encroached over the entire yard, after goods facilities were withdrawn. (D. Clayton)

17. The ridge finials and the gateway granite setts give an air of antiquity to this 1962 view. Two Consuls and an A35 would help to date the scene. (D. Cullum)

18. Transition in modernisation. The board-clad signal box and wooden crossing gates contrast in 1974 with the new materials of the up platform shelter and the additional foot-bridge. Colour light signals were introduced in April 1964, after which the box controlled the crossing only. (J. Scrace)

19. An up goods train on 15th August 1980 may look modern, being devoid of a brake van for the guard, but it actually has a number of now obsolete features. It has vac- uum brakes, wooden-sided wagons and formed the now extinct Eastleigh to Norwood Junction service. (J.A.M. Vaughan)

21. The 4SUB units were introduced in 1948-51 and served the stopping services on the line for over 30 years. The 17.02 Waterloo to Dorking is seen approaching the new flat-roofed station on the same day as the previous photograph. (J. Scrace)

20. Modern meets ultra-modern stock on 30th July 1981. The 16.50 Victoria to Bognor Regis, with unit no.7302 leading, speeds past the latest suburban EMU. Colour light sig-nals, lifting barriers and CCTV complete the transformation from the earlier views of this location. (J. Scrace)

LEATHERHEAD

22. Looking south from the down home signals in 1925, we see the former LSWR goods yard on the right and the ex LBSCR station and yard in the centre. The joint line and junction signal box are in the foreground. The box was the second one at this site, being erected in 1897. (Late E. Wallis)

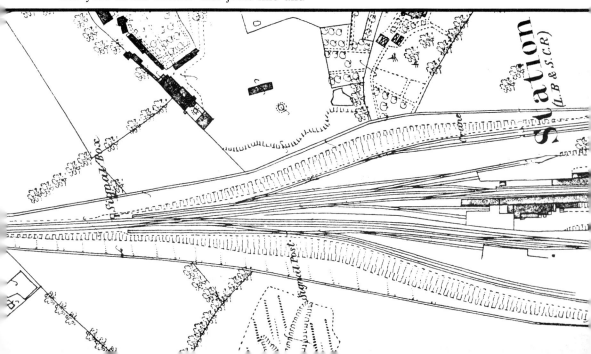

23. A southward view from the signals in the centre of the previous picture reveals three end-loading docks – two LBSCR and one LSWR. The former company's station is in the centre of the picture whilst its competitor's is beyond it, on the right. On the left is the LBSCR signal box, which is the only one of the three to remain in use in 1986. (Late E. Wallis)

The 1881 map shows LSWR station when it was a terminus, with the proposed extension to Effingham Junction drawn onto it. The first station was ½ mile to the north, just north of the Kingston Road. This was in use from 1st February 1859 until 3rd March 1867. The engine shed there continued to be used until 1874, when it was leased out as a church and school at £15 per annum. It survives today as an engineering works.

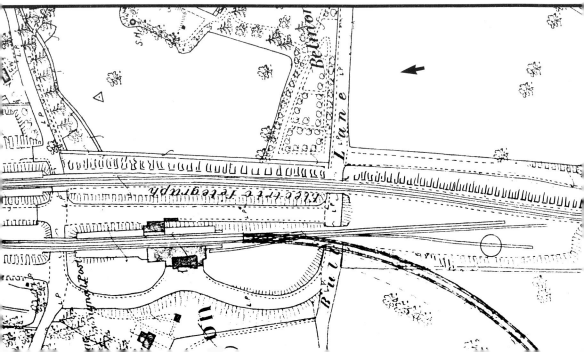

24. The final 1925 picture looks north from the down starting signal and shows the wooden platforms of the ex-LBSCR station on the right and ex-LSWR on the left. All of these were carried on bridges over the road to Cobham. (Late E. Wallis)

The 1914 map reveals fields still separating the town from its stations and a two-road engine shed, south of the turntable. The shed was built in 1903 and replaced a small one erected in 1885. It ceased to be used in 1927 and was demolished by 1932. The bold line shows the disused station approach area which was sold by the SR in 1934.

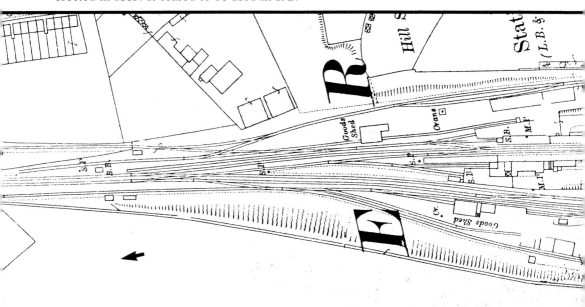

25. As at Epsom and Midhurst, the SR decided to alter the layout to avoid continuing to use two separate stations. Here it involved providing a new bridge over Station Road for

the Effingham Junction line. It is seen here, shortly before the former LSWR station (on the left) was abandoned on 10th July 1927. Spot the prostrate body. (British Rail)

26. Looking south from the down platform in 1960, the 1927 junction is apparent with a sub-station beyond it. Less obvious is the electric stock stabled in the remains of the LSWR station on the right. (D. Cullum)

27. A view in the opposite direction eight years later shows the differing styles of canopy valance and the extensive cycle shed on the up platform. (D. Cullum)

28. The LBSCR signal box on the down platform survives in 1986, although the boards have been panelled over. Its days are numbered as the influence of big panel boxes spreads. Photograph date – 18th April 1969. (J. Scrace)

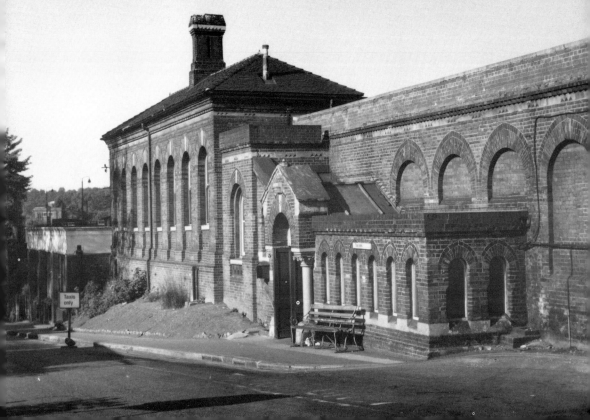

29. This fine facade with ornamental tower and polychromatic brickwork is on the up side. When photographed in 1973, the berthing sidings in the foreground were out of use, with the conductor rails lying in the "six-foot". (J. Scrace)

30. The multiplicity of arches on the down or town side cannot fail to impress. The decaying chimney has recently been carefully restored with matching bricks, as the station is now a listed structure. (J. Scrace)

31. Another 1975 view shows that the former LBSCR goods yard had partly been converted to a car park. At the north end there had once been sidings for the Gas Co. and the Faldo Asphalte Co. Only a single siding was retained for the Engineer's benefit. (J. Scrace)

33. The sudden emergence of the railway from a tunnel onto a viaduct is an alpine feature, enhanced in December 1978 by arctic weather. Two 4SUBs raise the fallen snow on their way from Victoria to Horsham, minus headcode. Sometimes the window froze shut, preventing the driver from reaching to position the stencil. (J.A.M. Vaughan)

32. Two miles south of Leatherhead, the line passes through Mickleham Tunnel and immediately crosses the River Mole. This is a beautiful location despite the presence of the A24 dual carriageway in the background. A grimy 4SUB rattles northward to Victoria, in 1978. (J.A.M. Vaughan)

34. As in the Arun Gap, the Downs presented a projection of chalk near a meander in the river, which necessitated the provision of a short tunnel. Leaving it on 16th April 1983 is a RCTS railtour from Victoria to Salisbury, hauled by nos.73142 *Broadlands* and 73129 *City of Winchester*. The coaches of the Venice Simplon Orient Express provided unusual luxury on the line. (J.A.M. Vaughan)

35. The route is almost straight for over three miles, including the 524yd tunnel. The 4COR units, with their characteristic swaying end gangways, provided the fast services to Bognor and Portsmouth for around 30 years. Mickleham Crossing gate is in the foreground. (D. Cullum collection)

36. The tiny crossing box, with its anti-downdraught flue pipe, ceased to function on 10th October 1971 and was soon removed. One of the conditions of sale of the land to the railway was that a crossing for Norbury Park House be provided and that all new buildings in the area should be painted green. (J. Scrace)

BOXHILL

37. There have been many changes of name. West Humble until 1870; Boxhill & Burford Bridge until 1896; plain Boxhill until 1904 and then Boxhill & Burford Bridge again. It is now Boxhill & West Humble. Here, staff emphasise that passengers are not allowed to cycle on the platform. (F.G. Holmes)

38. Although serving a thinly populated district, the station was busy in the summer with visitors to Box Hill, Ranmore Common and other beauty spots. The driver of this up London Bridge train has left his front windows open to improve ventilation in the heat of summer. (J. Harrod collection)

39. Two 1977 photographs highlight the architectural extravagance of the LBSCR's architect in a way that the passing passengers cannot appreciate. (J. Scrace)

40. A Victoria - Dorking train pauses briefly under the roofless footbridge. In 1986, the station was staffed part-time although the up side buildings were boarded up. No goods facilities have ever been provided here as Dorking is only one mile distant. (J. Scrace)

1935

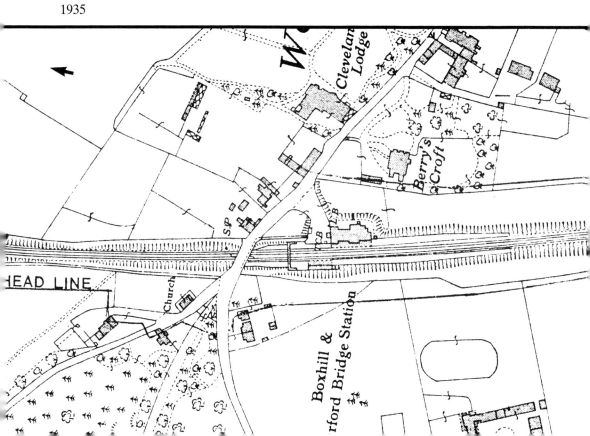

DORKING NORTH

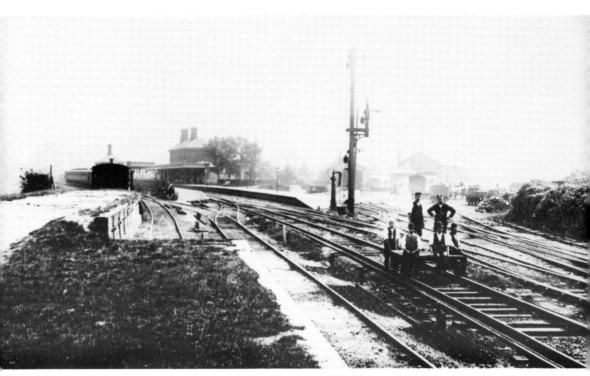

41. A rather poor print from 1893 shows two carriage sidings on the left (three more were added about 1900); an engine shed behind the signals and the goods yard on the right. (Late E. Wallis collection)

42. The exterior, seen from London Road in about 1906, presents a more restrained symmetrical style than those seen at the previous two stations. One of the signboard posts appears to be adorned with a signal finial. (Pamlin Prints)

43. Points of interest in this splendid but undated photograph are the uniforms, the advertisements, the matching canopies and the signal box in the distance.
(Lens of Sutton)

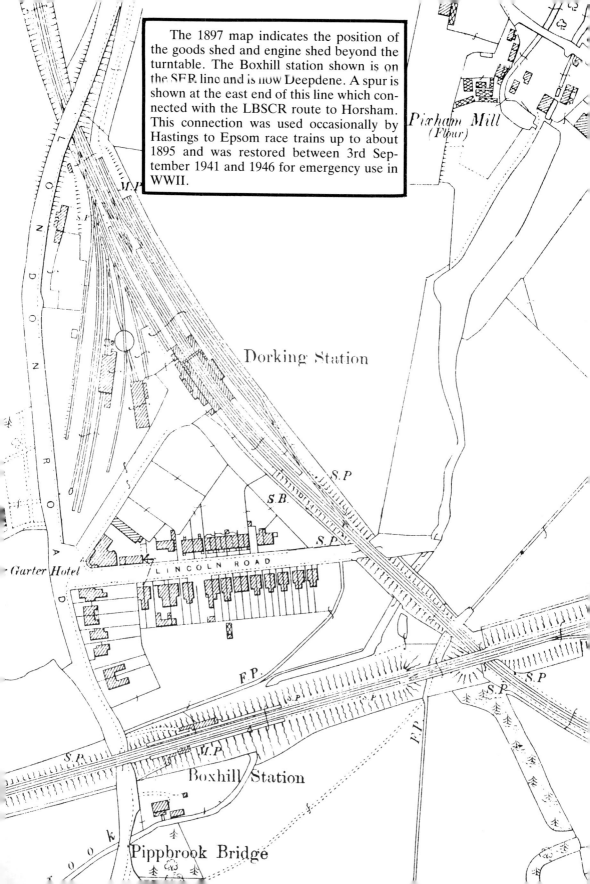

The 1897 map indicates the position of the goods shed and engine shed beyond the turntable. The Boxhill station shown is on the SER line and is now Deepdene. A spur is shown at the east end of this line which connected with the LBSCR route to Horsham. This connection was used occasionally by Hastings to Epsom race trains up to about 1895 and was restored between 3rd September 1941 and 1946 for emergency use in WWII.

Pixham Mill
(Flour)

Dorking Station

S.P

S.B.

S.P.

Garter Hotel

LINCOLN ROAD

F.P.

S.P.

S.P

S.P.

F.P

S.P.

M.P.

Boxhill Station

Pippbrook Bridge

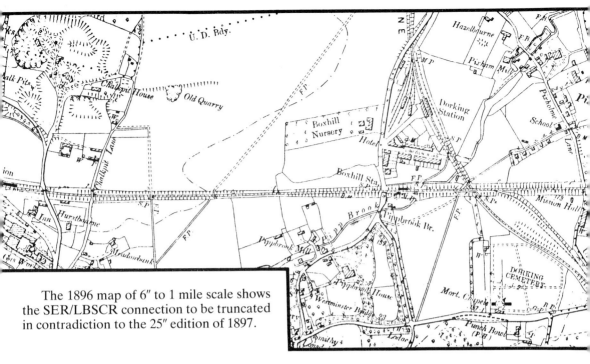

The 1896 map of 6″ to 1 mile scale shows the SER/LBSCR connection to be truncated in contradiction to the 25″ edition of 1897.

44. Class D1 0–4–2T no.291 *Deepdene* blows off as she heads for London with seven bogies. The signalman looks down on four other locomotives in the goods yard and one wonders if this was a regular feature of operations. (Bluebell Archives)

45. A less sharp picture shows another D1, no.19 *Belmont*, waiting to depart northwards, whilst some minor track work is carried out in the up bay. The locomotive was scrapped in 1913, which helps to date the photograph. (D. Cullum collection)

47. No.6 was of class I1, a classification intended to confuse typesetters. The class remained unnamed, except by enginemen disapproving of their performance. Beyond the bowler hats on the up platform is the stable block that housed the company's cartage horses. (Bluebell Archives)

46. *Dorking* at Dorking! Elegant 229 poses in front of beautiful Box Hill, whilst the fireman trims the coal. This engine ran from 1884 until 1947. (Bluebell Archives)

48. A porter waits to cross the lines with passengers' cases as an up freight plods through. Behind him, the down canopy supports a remarkable number of gas lights. (Lens of Sutton)

49. Signalman P. Funnell was able to see over the road bridge from his high 31-lever box, erected in 1877 and photographed in 1922. The original box had been on the up platform, south of the station, and was retained until 1926 as a shunting box. (Late E. Wallis)

50. An historic moment – the first electric train, on 9th July 1925 – a week before public services commenced. The platform is yet to be tarmaced. (R. Randell collection)

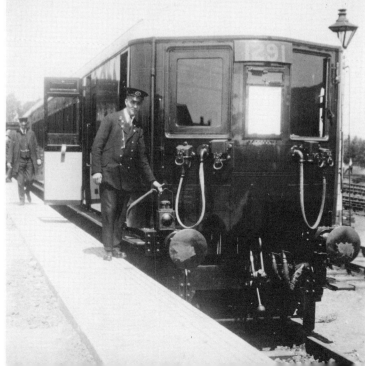

51. A digression for signalling students – in the foreground is the up intermediate starting signal in 1927, with tapered arm and a rotary replacer on the post, and in the background we see the starting signals – up bay, up main and down loop up. (Late E. Wallis)

53. Ex-LSWR class T9 4–4–0 no.E311 waits to restart a Victoria to Bognor Regis express, in about 1932. The matching canopy for the new down platform is evident on the right. The electrified line at this platform terminated at buffers at the south end, until 1938. (Dr. I.C. Allen)

52. Further south, the down advanced starter had been fitted with an SR pattern "shunt into forward section" signal by December 1927. The bridge carries the Redhill - Guildford line. (Late E. Wallis)

54. Between 1925 and 1938, a local service was provided on the non-electrified line between Dorking and Horsham by push-pull units. Here we see class E5 no.2401 with two ex-LSWR coaches, converted for railmotor working, in June 1933. (Dr. I.C. Allen)

56. Looking south in 1969, the six electrified carriage sidings are evident and the engineers have acquired the goods yard, which closed in 1964. The engine shed had been damaged in a gale and was demolished in the early 1920s. (J. Scrace)

55. An August 1960 view shows the third bridge span which was provided to allow lengthening of the island platform and carriage sidings. In the distance, a Redhill-bound train is leaving Deepdene station. (D. Clayton)

57. Unit no.4661 was damaged when no.4745, forming the 15.21 Horsham to Waterloo, was in collision when attaching to it on 3rd September 1973. At that time, all three platform canopies were intact.
(J. Scrace)

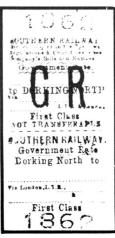

58. By 1978, the down main platform had lost its weather protection. By 1982, the up side buildings had been completely reconstructed and the intricate cast iron stanchion brackets, seen here, were scrapped. (J. Scrace)

SOUTHERN RY.
Training Scheme.

SOUTHERN RY.
Training Scheme.

Available on or before
31st December 1924.
One journey only.

Available on or before
31st December 1924.
One journey only.

DORKING to
ANY STATION in
Northern District.

ANY STATION in
Northern District
to DORKING

THIRD CL. [FREE
is Ticket must be presented at the Book.
Office to be dated on the day intended to be u

THIRD CL. [FREE

0483   0483

BRITISH RAILWAYS (S)
This ticket is issued subject to the Bye-laws,
Regulations and Conditions contained in the
Publications and Notices of an l applicable to the
Railway Executive.

Walking & Cycling Tourist.
Available the Month including Day of issue.

Dorking North to

Via

THIRD CLASS
NOT TRANSFERABLE

0063

59. On 28th August 1983, no.1 siding contained the preserved 4SUB unit repainted in
Southern green livery and no.3 platform
accommodated a class 508 EMU. These units
were introduced in 1979 and ceased to oper-
ate the route in October 1984, when they
were transferred to Merseyside.
(P.G. Barnes)

60. Ex-Metropolitan Railway electric locomotive *Sarah Siddons* leaves platform 2 with "The Mary Rose" railtour from Portsmouth, on 7th July 1984. One can also study the 1938 Odeon-style signal box; the modern carriage siding lighting system; the recent building developments on platform 1 and the lack of change on platform 3. (J. Scrace)

61. No.204 *Telford* climbs up the 1 in 90 gradient in about 1910 and runs over the junction of the former spur to the SER. This was retained as a siding until about 1926, the unused land thereabouts being used for the storage of hay collected from the lineside elsewhere. (S.C. Nash collection)

62. Class B4 no.52 heads south, with the hay siding rising behind the train and the SECR signals and bridge visible in the distance. The allotments indicate that it is summertime and so no hay ricks would be present. The company still required substantial quantities of fodder for its numerous cartage horses and also some shunting horses.
(E.R. Lacey collection)

63. An up mineral train passes under the Reigate road (now A24), as it descends the 1 in 80 incline behind class E3 no.165. (Lens of Sutton)

64. An up express from Bognor Regis leaves the 384yd Betchworth Tunnel, behind class I3 4–4–2T no.2091, just prior to electrification. This tunnel is through sand – the direct line to Portsmouth similarly passes through two tunnels – one in chalk and the next in sand, south of Guildford. (S.C. Nash)

65. Another view of the extinct Eastleigh - Norwood Junction freight in August 1980. The tunnel partially collapsed on 27th February 1877, but with less serious consequences than the collapse of one of the Guildford tunnels in 1895. See our *Woking to Portsmouth* album – picture no.31 for details. (J.A.M. Vaughan)

66. Lodge Farm crossing is 2½ miles south of Betchworth Tunnel at the foot of the 1 in 100 climb to Holmwood. In consequence of the gradients, catch points were provided either side of the box in the days of loose coupled goods trains. The 1877 box ceased to be a block post after electrification and its four levers stopped work altogether in January 1986. (J. Scrace)

HOLMWOOD

68. Unlike the other stations on the route, Holmwood was built on a bridge across the track. Convenient for passengers but not for handling parcels of the dimensions of the one on the trap. The entrance to the goods yard was 200yds down the hill.
(P. Brackpool collection)

1896. Why the cartographer showed three signal boxes is a mystery.

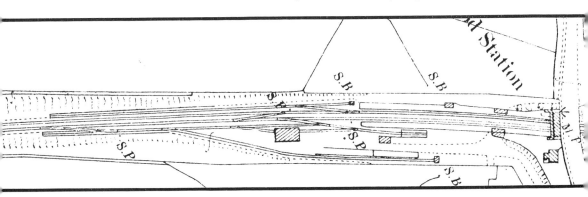

67. One of the class H1 Marsh Atlantics climbs towards Holmwood, whilst an official observes progress from the end window of the leading clerestory coach. The Royal Train was possibly bound for Singleton for Goodwood Races. The locomotive was definitely built by Kitson & Co. in 1906.
(Lens of Sutton)

69. Signalman Grantham poses by his acetylene-lit bicycle, three days after the SR had been created. The space under the timber platform was known as the "lead-away". (Late E. Wallis)

70. Looking south in 1923, we can appreciate the size of the goods shed, the extent of the goods yard and the staithes for domestic coal. Gunpowder vans often appeared in the yard, bringing materials for the nearby Schermuly Pistol Rocket Works where the "Verey Light" signal flares were made.
(Late E. Wallis)

71. Looking in the opposite direction, we gain a good view of the cattle dock (pens in the foreground) and can see the position of the drive up to the main road, parallel to the station master's underclothes.
(Late E. Wallis)

72. At Dorking it was necessary to have a tall signal box to see over the bridge – the reverse applied here. Class I1X no. B595 comes to a standstill, in 1927, opposite one of the curious LBSCR three-wheeled milk barrows, examples of which can be seen today on the Bluebell Railway. (Dr. I.C. Allen)

Bradshaw 1890

Fares.] LEATHERHEAD, EPSOM, WIMBLEDON, and LONDON.—London & South Western.

Week Days / Sundays timetable. Stations (downward):

	1 cl.	2 cl.	3 cl.	Week Days													Sundays			
Mls	s.d.	s.d.	s.d.		mrn	mrn	mrn	mrn	mrn	mrn	aft	aft	aft	aft	aft	aft	mrn	aft	aft	aft
—				Leatherhead..dep																
1½	0 4	0 3	0 1½	Ashtead																
3½	0 8	0 6	0 3½	Epsom																
4½	0 10	0 8	0 5	Ewell																
7	1 4	1 0	0 7	Worcester Park																
9	1 8	1 3	0 9	Raynes Park 41																
10½	2 2	1 6	0 10½	Wimbledon 41																
12	2 6	1 10	1 0½	Earlsfield *																
13½	2 6	2 0	1 2	Clapham Junc. 56																
17	3 0	2 6	1 5	66 Kensington ar																
16½	3 0	2 6	1 4½	Vauxhall																
17½	3 0	2 6	1 6	Waterloo ....arr																

LONDON, WIMBLEDON, EPSOM, and LEATHERHEAD.—L. & S. W.

Fares.			Week Days.										Sundays
1 cl.	2 cl.	3 cl.		mrn	mrn	mrn	aft	aft	aft	aft	aft	mrn	aft aft aft
			Waterloo....dep										
0 8	0 6	0 4	Vauxhall										
0 8	0 6	0 4	66 Kensington d										
0 6	0 4	0 3	Clapham Junc.										
0 9	0 7	0 5	Earlsfield *										
1 4	1 0	0 7	Wimbledon										
1 8	1 2	0 8½	Raynes Park										
1 9	1 3	0 10½	Worcester Park										
2 0	1 6	1 0½	Ewell										
2 3	1 9	1 2	Epsom 83										
2 6	2 0	1 4	Ashtead										
3 0	2 6	1 6	Leatherhead 68										

* Earlsfield and Summer's Town. b Start from Central Station, Waterloo.

73. A photographic study taken to illustrate the phrase "reading between the lines". The station master's son sits on the barrow crossing on 29th May 1937, his home being visible, close to his right ear. (J.D. Knight)

74. BR class 4 no.73022 speeds south with an RCTS railtour on 28th March 1963, the year before the goods yard was closed. The crane remains but the goods shed had been demolished in 1958, as it had become unsafe. (J. Scrace)

75. The solitary up siding had been electrified in 1938 and for many years a London stopping service terminated here every hour, being berthed in the siding during layover. A cat walk was provided to assist crews changing ends and it can be seen in the background of this 1969 view. The siding was lengthened 10 feet in 1961, to accommodate the EPB units, and ceased to be used after the Autumn of 1976. (J. Scrace)

76. In 1968 the roof of the footbridge was removed and later much of the station was boarded up, as can be seen in this 1981 photograph. In 1986 access to the platforms was via the goods yard as the buildings had been declared unsafe and even the signal box was not manned regularly. (J.A.M. Vaughan)

OCKLEY

77. The driver of class D1 *Bonchurch* looks at Junior Porter Sid Dawes, standing proudly beside his drop-handlebars in 1922. This was the highest non-terminal station on the LBSCR. (Lens of Sutton)

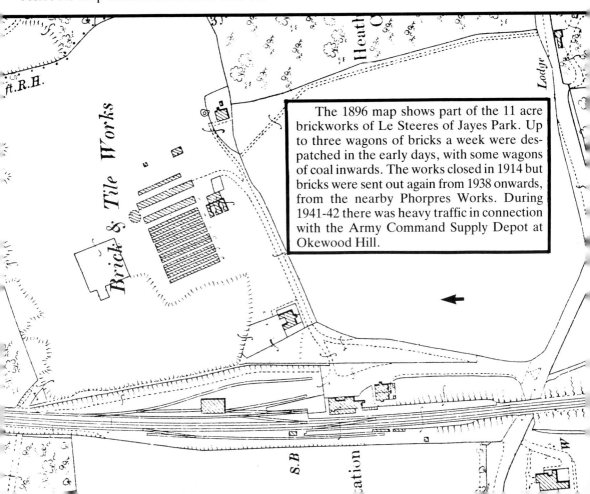

ft.R.H.

Brick & Tile Works

Heath

Lodge

The 1896 map shows part of the 11 acre brickworks of Le Steeres of Jayes Park. Up to three wagons of bricks a week were despatched in the early days, with some wagons of coal inwards. The works closed in 1914 but bricks were sent out again from 1938 onwards, from the nearby Phorpres Works. During 1941-42 there was heavy traffic in connection with the Army Command Supply Depot at Okewood Hill.

S.B

78. The single up siding on the right was used for milk traffic but as this was lost to road transport the line was lifted in 1932, nine years after this photograph was taken. The yard on the left received general goods and household coal and sent out hay, grain, faggots, cordwood, pea-boughs and bean sticks. (Late E. Wallis)

80. Class E5X no.2570, formerly *Armington*, stands over the subway, the iron roof of which caused gaps to be left in the conductor rails. The new lamp post by the cycle shed was about to receive electric light, which would date the scene as 1938. (Lens of Sutton)

79. The original signal box was replaced in 1877 and was superseded by this one in January 1905. It had 22 levers and is seen on 1st June 1923 with Signalman R. Brewer in charge. A porch was added in 1956 but the box was closed in 1965, being demolished two years later. (Late E. Wallis)

81. The station is surrounded by fields to this day, and is over one mile from Capel and 1½ from Ockley. The white panel is a "modesty screen", erected in front of the entrance to the Gents in 1956. This pleasant scene was recorded in July 1969. (J. Scrace)

82. In 1981, the exterior presented a neglected look, having lost its canopy about 10 years earlier. The letter box in the wall and the gate to the goods yard (which closed in June 1962) serve as a reminder of the importance of the location in bygone days. (D. Cullum)

83. This memorial bush is on the down side, about two miles south of Ockley and local legend relates that it was planted and tended in memory of a ganger who was struck by a locomotive whilst walking to Northwood up distant, for fog signalling duty. (P. Brackpool)

84. Built in 1899 as an intermediate block post to meet increasing traffic, it had only four levers in use and was manned only at peak times of the day until 1927, after which it was used on Bank Holidays primarily. Entomologist signalmen would have enjoyed working the box as it was always full of insects and flies of various types. The machine room window was never repaired, as this would have disturbed the nesting routines of some local house martins. The box was over two miles to the adjacent stations and ceased to be used after 1956. Note the stile over the lineside cables in this 1965 photograph, taken a year before the box was demolished. (J. Scrace)

WARNHAM

85. The first brickworks hereabouts was started in the field on the left of this 1923 picture, in 1890 by Mr. Peter Peters. The bricks were burnt in clamps, not kilns, and the site was served by a branch of the up siding which curved away at right angles to the main line.

It commenced by the far lamp post and ran behind and parallel to the eight pairs of cottages, shown on the maps and the next photograph. These were built by the enterprising Mr. Peters when demand for bricks was low. (Late E. Wallis)

1897

Warnham

S.P.

Brick Yard

86. Up to 12 wagons of London's rubbish per week arrived to fill the clay pits but Mr. Peter's men first removed any cinders or partially burnt coal for use as fuel in brick-making! He sold his business to Mr. Belcher in 1898, who soon built brick kilns on the opposite side of the railway. Three sidings were eventually laid to the works, the chimneys of which are visible in this 1923 view. (Late E. Wallis)

87. The 1877 signal box had 20 levers and a gate wheel was added later. Signalman Bert Sandell, a loyal LBSCR man, was photographed in February 1923 wearing a cloth cap as he refused to wear his new SR one. (Late E. Wallis)

J. MITCHELL,
WARNHAM STATION,
Nr. HORSHAM, SUSSEX.

ONE: HORSHAM 313.   PHONE: HORSHAM

14 Seater   and   20 Seater Cars   1 Ton Lorries
                                    For Hire.

88. In 1912 James Mitchell bought the shop seen to the left of the station in photograph no.86. Behind it, there were coal staithes adjacent to the brickfield siding, from which he operated his coal business. In 1921, his horse and cart was replaced by a model T Ford one-ton lorry. On Saturdays, it was swept out, fitted with a canvas cover and makeshift seats. Thus the first bus service to Horsham commenced and the railway had a competitor. In 1922, a second model T Ford operated to Ockley every weekday, and by about 1925 services had expanded so as to require the fleet illustrated. A sting in the tail was a toll charged by the SR for the use of *their* Station Road. Bus services ceased in 1969. (W. Walker collection)

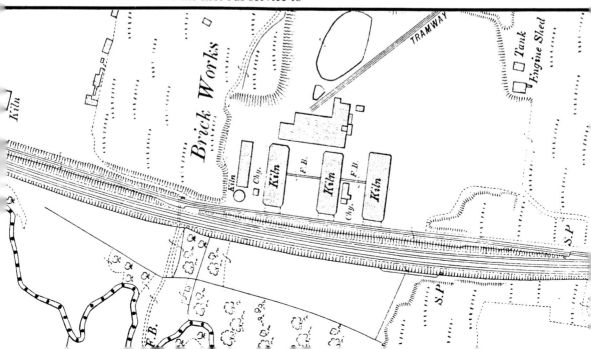

89. Bricks are stacked on the platform in 1960 ready to repair the damaged doorway in the goods shed. A similar accident befell Horsham shed, years earlier, when a wagon flap had been left down on the dock. Goods services ceased in 1964 and the shed was demolished. (D. Cullum collection)

1912

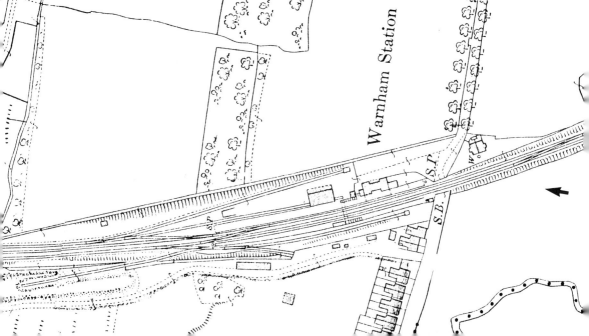

90. The 17.02 Waterloo to Horsham arrives on 11th July 1969. The following year, the remaining porter was made redundant and thereafter the signalman issued the tickets. (J. Scrace)

91. A view from the up starting signal on the same day shows the former goods yard stocked with road-borne coal by A.P. Wakeford and the yard on the right still occupied by Mitchells. (J. Scrace)

92. On 15th May 1971, no. E6043 passes through with an unusual Newhaven to Leatherhead special. The shed with steeply pitched roof, beyond the sleeper-built PW hut on the left, housed a water pump until mains arrived in 1935. It was worked, by hand, by a junior member of staff each day, to supply all the station's needs. (J. Scrace)

93. The east elevation in 1972 retained its canopy and displayed its two-tone brickwork. The chimney stacks and pots show much variety. (J. Scrace)

94. The crossovers were removed shortly after this photograph was taken in 1978. A Saturdays-only freight service was operated to the sidings from Horsham by a diesel-electric shunter, from 1964 until January 1970. (P. Brackpool)

95. Up to a dozen wagons of Sherwood slack from the Nottinghamshire coalfields arrived each week and numerous wagon loads of bricks were consigned to the London suburbs and the Brighton - Worthing area in particular. By 1979, nature was taking over. (P. Brackpool)

96. On 5th May 1984, no.33059 was forced to run "wrong line" with the Horsham - Ince UKF Fertiliser empty van train, due to a land slip blocking the up line near Ockley. The crossover in the distance remained in place in 1986. (P.G. Barnes)

97. The same train is again subjected to single line working and hand signalling, behind 33001 on 22nd January 1983. The props visible at the back of the signal box have been in place for many years. The lane leading to the main road (²⁄₃ mile) was built by the LBSCR at a cost of £1600 and the lane eastwards from the station (¼ mile) was constructed by the owner of Graylands Estate in 1898-99. It remained a private road until 1961. (J.A.M. Vaughan)

98. The lofty Junction Box stood sentinel over the divergence of the lines from 1875 to 1938. The Three Bridges route disappears in the distance whilst the Dorking tracks follow the white signal wire posts to the left. (D. Cullum collection)

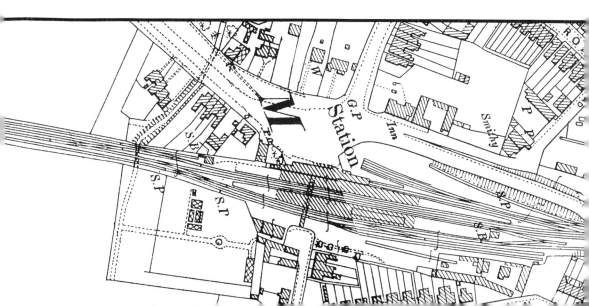

99. A post card from about 1920 shows the station on the left and a house on the right with stone slab roofing, a material restricted to the Horsham district. It is ½ mile from the town centre to the station (D. Cullum collection)

The cartographer of the 1897 edition was in error in failing to show connections between the main line and the engine shed lines and the short siding east of the station. The 1876 map and numerous other photographs of this location appear in our *Branch Lines to Horsham*.

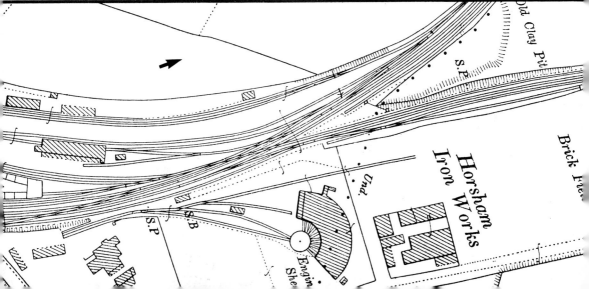

100. The other two signal boxes are visible in this view – "West" in the distance and "Shunting Box" on the right. The first goods shed was demolished about 1875 to make way for the widening of the down platform to form an island platform. The Carfax (town centre) is beyond the church spire. (Lens of Sutton)

101. The goods staff pose in front of class E1 no.98 in about 1905. The locomotive was scrapped in 1913. Behind it are the sawmills of J & S Agate, who were provided with a siding in 1884 at a rental of £1 per annum. (Late E. Wallis collection)

102. A down train drifts past Shunting Box, opposite which the signals have their lamps separate from the arms. The first station was a terminus on the north side of the main road, as at Leatherhead. Similarly, a bridge for the road had to be built before the line could be extended to a new station.
(D. Cullum collection)

Station and Signal Box.	Distance from next Box above. M.	Yds.	Position.	WEEK DAYS. Open.	Closed.	SUNDAYS. Open.	Closed.
Epsom Town— Station	1	98	Down side, Eas end	5.0 a.m. Mons.	—	—	12.0 midt.
L. & S.W. BOXES. Epsom, L. & S.W.— Epsom Junc. (East	–	646	East end of Up Platform ...	5.15 a.m.	1.15 a.m.	7.30 a.m.	11.30 p.m.
Epsom Junc (West)	–	424	West end of Up Platform ...				
Epsom Common ...	–	1,403	Down side	3.50 p.m.	6.0 p.m.	Closed	—
Ashtead— Station	1	106	Centre of Up Platform	5.15 a.m.	1.15 a.m.	7.30 a.m.	11.30 p.m.
Leatherhead L.&S.W. Ashtead Woods ...	–	1,304	Up side	7.30 a.m.	5.30 p.m.	Closed	—
Junction	–	1,511	Down side	5.15 a.m.	1.15 a.m.	7.45 a.m.	11.45 p.m.
Leatherhead— Station	–	297	West end of Down Platform ...	6.0 a.m. Monday	— —	— 7.45 a.m.	6.0 a.m. 11.15 p.m.

1922

Station and Signal Box.	Distance from next Box above. M.	Yds.	Position.	WEEK DAYS. Open.	Closed.	SUNDAYS. Open.	Closed.
Box Hill—							
Mickleham Crossing ...	2	356	Up side, S. end of Tunnel.	As ordered in Special Traffic Notice			
Station	-	1,642	North end of Up Platform.	6.30 a.m.	9.0 p.m.	Closed	
Dorking—							
Station	-	1,516	Up side entrance to Goods Yard, North of Station.	6.0 a.m. Mondays	—	—	11.0 p.m.
Tilehurst Lane	1	1,686	Down Side	As ordered in Special Traffic Notice			
Holmwood							
Lodge Farm Crossing .	1	947	Down side	7.0 a.m.	10.0 p.m.	Closed	
Station	1	1,030	Middle of Platform on Up side.	{ 6.0 a.m. { Mondays	—	{ — { 7.0 a.m. { 6.30 p.m.	{ 6.0 a.m. { 11.30a.m. { 9.0 p.m. }
Oakley—							
Station	2	239	North end of Up Platform.	{ 6.0 a.m. { Mondays }	—	{ — { 6.0 p.m.	{ 11.0 a.m. { 9.0 p.m. }
Northwood	2	107	Down side	{ 10.45a.m. { 2.15p.m.	12.30p.m { 7.45p.m }	Closed	—
Warnham—							
Station	2	594	South end of Up Platform.	7.0 a.m.	10.15 p.m.	{ 8.0 a.m. { 6.30 p.m.	{ 1. 0 p.m. { 9. 0 p.m. }

1922

103. The first locomotive shed had three roads, its location being shown on the 1876 map. This semi-roundhouse replaced it in 1896 and had 10 bays. A further eight bays were added about four years later. Class D1 no.237 is standing on the 46ft turntable. (A.B. McLeod/R.C. Riley collection)

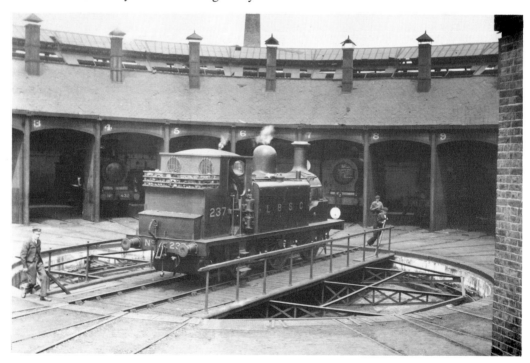

104. The platforms were lengthened in the mid-1870s and a level crossing at the south end eliminated. New canopies were also pro- vided – the previous one on the down platform had been attached to the goods shed wall. (Lens of Sutton)

105. Looking north-east from the road bridge in about 1924, we see the second goods shed (right of centre) which, by then, had lost the awning shown in picture no.98. It was demolished in 1926. On the left is the granary. (Late E. Wallis)

106. An up bay platform was provided in 1865, being lengthened and realigned about 10 years later. Class D1 no.2254 stands in it, probably awaiting departure to Dorking. (Lens of Sutton)

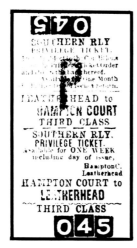

108. In 1938 the station was totally reconstructed. On the left, the previous building is represented by a heap of rubble; the subway filled in and this temporary footbridge was erected. The electric train consists of two 3-car sets, with two ex-steam coaches between them, and is seen two weeks after electrification. (H.C. Casserley)

107. Class E5 no.2399, *Middleton* in LBSCR days, retards its short train, as it enters the down loop sometime prior to electrification. In the background are Agate's sheer legs. (Lens of Sutton)

109. The three 1875 signal boxes were introduced to end the dangerous time interval system. This box was brought into use on 24th April 1938 to displace all three. It remains in use today, controlling colour light signals. (F.G. Holmes)

111. A Princes Risborough to Bognor Regis Excursion passes the scene of the accident, on 28th June 1959, hauled by class U1 no.31894. The siding was electrified in 1944, following the introduction of electric locomotives nos. CC1 and CC2. (J. Scrace)

110. On 30th May 1957, the Norwood Junction goods train was leaving the yard but the driver of class C2X no.32543 was on the wrong side of the engine to see the ground signal. He asked his fireman to report on it but there was a misunderstnding and the train ran through the head shunt buffers, into Wimblehurst Road. (J. Scrace)

112. The shed was in decline when photographed on 19th July 1959, with class E4 no.32475 standing by the shed staff lobby. In August 1960 it became a sub-shed to Three Bridges and was closed completely on 1st January 1965. (J. Scrace)

113. On the same day, three 4COR units swing round the curve from Dorking, bound for the South Coast. In the nearby siding, two eras of agriculture are coupled together – a horse box and a combine harvester, the latter still novel in those days. (J. Scrace)

114. The weeds rise six months after the closure of the shed. The electric coaling crane had been supplied in 1954 and the 55ft turntable had been brought from Orpington in 1927. The site was cleared in 1971. (J. Scrace)

Bradshaw 1890

LONDON and CROYDON to EPSOM, DORKING, and HOLMWOOD.—L. B. & S. C.

115. Not a route indication – just the age of the driver. Leading Driver Charlie Scrace of Horsham removes the stencil headcode for the last time to celebrate his 65th birthday and retirement on 23rd October 1966. (J. Scrace)

117. The 17.22 Waterloo to Horsham clatters past Agate's timber yard on 1st June 1983, during the last week of operation of 4SUBs. Industrial premises have spread over the engine shed site, behind the signal box by coach six. (J. Scrace)

116. A 4SUB for Waterloo waits in the down loop on 11th June 1982, whilst a 4EPB stands in the up loop, which was created in the 1938 alterations. In 1943, the Home Guard positioned 20mm cannons on the roof of the footbridge and the signal box. (J. Scrace)

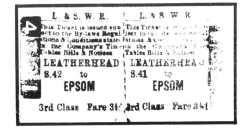

118. The driver of 33058 correctly checks his train of fertiliser vans as he leaves the yard on 16th April 1983. UKF established a depot on the north side of the yard in 1970, six years after general goods traffic ceased. (J. Scrace)

120. A class O8 diesel shunter stands on the left in an area now devoted to storage of lineside electrical equipment. A pair of class 508 units arrive on 1st July 1983. In 1986, most services to London via Epsom are worked by class 455 units and although the journey time is longer the scenery is most enjoyable and even spectacular in the vicinity of Box Hill. (J. Scrace)

119. Whilst an EPB unit for Dorking stands at platform 4, the Sandite train, composed of a former 2HAL unit, waits on the down main line. Sandite is an antidote to the slimy film formed on rails in the Autumn by fallen leaves which gives rise to braking problems and flat tyres. (P.G. Barnes)

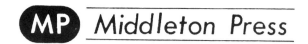

Easebourne Lane, Midhurst, West Sussex, GU29 9AZ
☎ Midhurst (073 081) 3169

BRANCH LINES

BRANCH LINES TO MIDHURST	0 906520 01 0
BRANCH LINES TO HORSHAM	0 906520 02 9
BRANCH LINE TO SELSEY	0 906520 04 5
BRANCH LINES TO EAST GRINSTEAD	0 906520 07 X
BRANCH LINES TO ALTON	0 906520 11 8
BRANCH LINE TO HAYLING	0 906520 12 6
BRANCH LINE TO SOUTHWOLD	0 906520 15 0
BRANCH LINE TO TENTERDEN	0 906520 21 5
BRANCH LINES TO NEWPORT	0 906520 26 6

SOUTH COAST RAILWAYS

BRIGHTON TO WORTHING	0 906520 03 7
WORTHING TO CHICHESTER	0 906520 06 1
CHICHESTER TO PORTSMOUTH	0 906520 14 2
BRIGHTON TO EASTBOURNE	0 906520 16 9
RYDE TO VENTNOR	0 906520 19 3
EASTBOURNE TO HASTINGS	0 906520 27 4

SOUTHERN MAIN LINES

WOKING TO PORTSMOUTH	0 906520 25 8
HAYWARDS HEATH TO SEAFORD	0 906520 28 2

STEAMING THROUGH

STEAMING THROUGH KENT	0 906520 13 4
STEAMING THROUGH EAST HANTS	0 906520 18 5
STEAMING THROUGH EAST SUSSEX	0 906520 22 3

OTHER RAILWAY BOOKS

INDUSTRIAL RAILWAYS OF THE SOUTH-EAST	0 906520 09 6
WAR ON THE LINE The official history of the SR in World War II	0 906520 10 X
GARRAWAY FATHER AND SON The story of two careers in steam	0 906520 20 7

OTHER BOOKS

MIDHURST TOWN – THEN & NOW	0 906520 05 3
EAST GRINSTEAD – THEN & NOW	0 906520 17 7
THE GREEN ROOF OF SUSSEX A refreshing amble along the South Downs Way	0 906520 08 8
THE MILITARY DEFENCE OF WEST SUSSEX	0 906520 23 1
WEST SUSSEX WATERWAYS	0 906520 24 X
BATTLE OVER PORTSMOUTH A City at war in 1940	0 906520 29 0